HOW TO DRAW

Not everyone is an artist. . .but almost anyone can learn to draw by following step-by-step instructions. If you can draw a fairly good circle freehand (you can practice first!), you can draw the characters in this book. And with lots of experience, who knows? You may become an artist after all.

You will need a good drawing surface. Use strong paper with a slightly rough surface (like the paper in this book). Pencils clip on a surface which is shiny; erasers make holes in paper that is too thin.

Pencils with medium-soft lead work the best (e.g. No. 2). Have a pencil sharpener handy to keep points sharp. A ruler will help you draw straight lines. Be sure to have a good eraser. Add a good light source and you're ready to begin.

Circles, ovals and pears are shapes used most often in drawing. Lines for neck, arms and legs form a simple skeleton to hold the shapes together. Always start drawings by *lightly* sketching the basic shapes.

Now let's get started. You can work right in this book on the spaces provided on each page. There are extra blank pages in the back of the book for more practice. Have fun!

HOUSE PETS

DRAW THE BASIC SHAPE OF THE CAT.

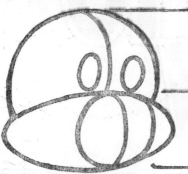

ADD DETAIL.

POINTED EARS

NOSE AND MOUTH

THE ADULT CAT IS 3 HEADS HIGH.

1.

2.

3.

1.

2.

3.

DRAW THE BASIC HEAD SHAPE FOR THE KITTEN.

ADD BIG POINTED EARS,

EYES, NOSÉ AND MOUTH.

THE KITTEN IS 2 HEADS HIGH.

1.

2.

1.

2.

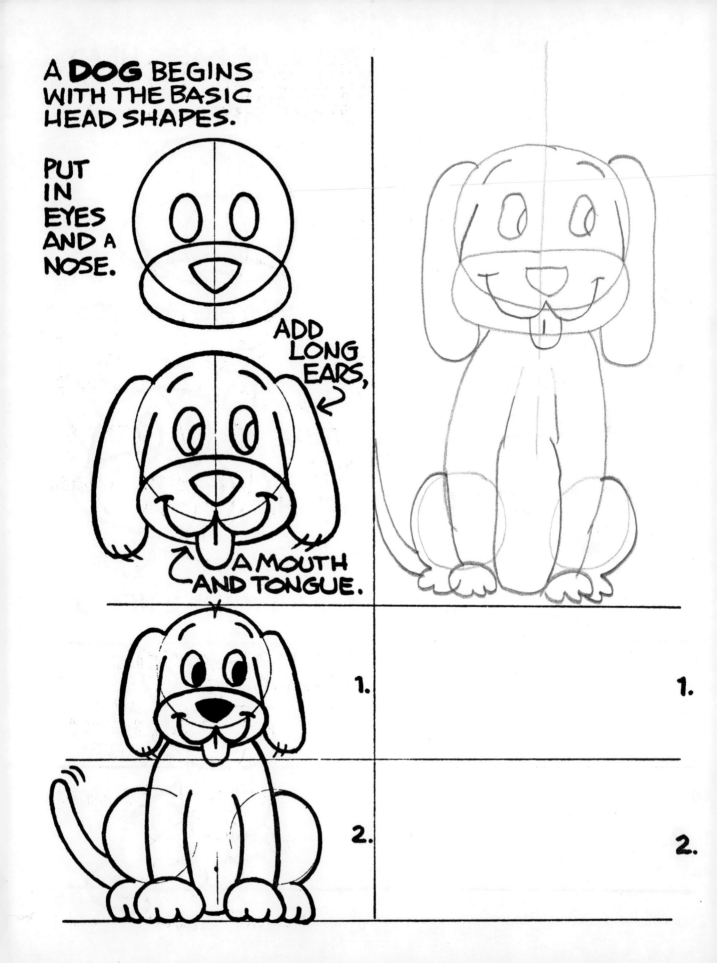

A **DOG** BEGINS WITH THE BASIC HEAD SHAPES.

PUT IN EYES AND A NOSE.

ADD LONG EARS,

A MOUTH AND TONGUE.

1.

2.

1.

2.

TO DRAW A **PUPPY** START WITH THE BASIC HEAD SHAPE.

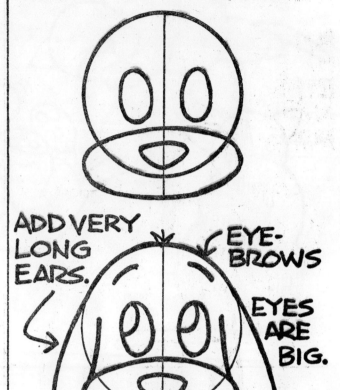

ADD VERY LONG EARS.

EYE-BROWS

EYES ARE BIG.

THE PUPPIE'S HEAD IS VERY BIG,

AND IT GROWS INTO ITS FEET!

CATS CAN BE PLAYFUL OR QUIET!

DOGS IN ACTION !

JUST CHANGE
THE EARS
AND HAIR.

FARM ANIMALS

TO DRAW A **HORSE**,
BEGIN WITH THE
BASIC SHAPES.

ADD THE NOSTRILS,
EARS AND MANE.

THE HORSE
HAS A LONG
NOSE.

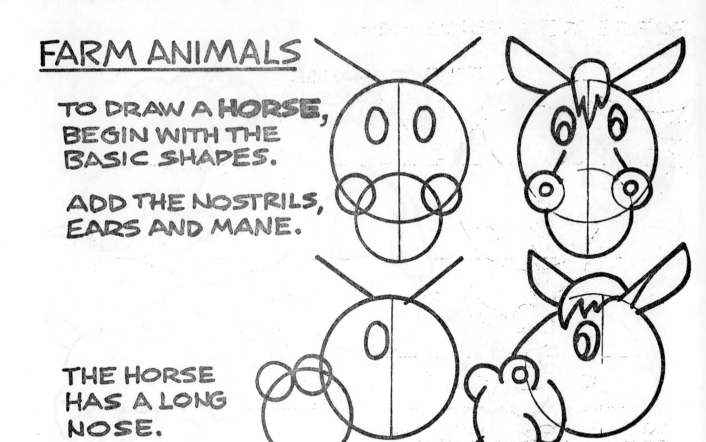

HORSE IS 3½ HEADS HIGH.

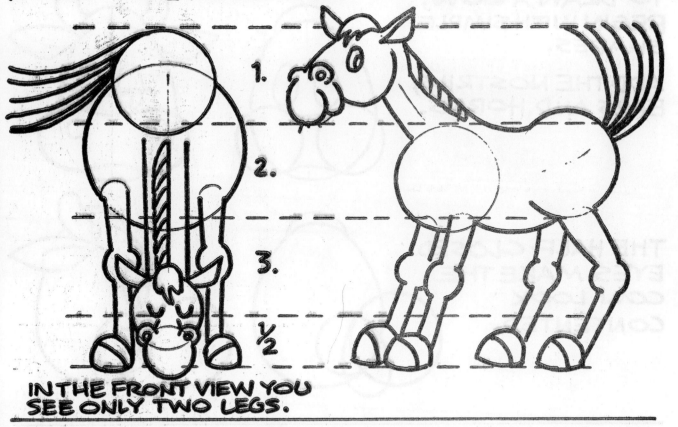

1.

2.

3.

½

IN THE FRONT VIEW YOU
SEE ONLY TWO LEGS.

1.

2.

3.

½

TO DRAW A **COW**,
BEGIN WITH SIMPLE
SHAPES.

ADD THE NOSTRILS,
EARS AND HORNS.

THE HALF-CLOSED
EYES MAKE THE
COW LOOK
CONTENTED.

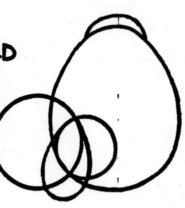

1.

2.

3.

THE COW IS ABOUT 3 HEADS
TALL AND 3 HEADS LONG.

1.

2.

3.

TO DRAW THE **CHICKEN**, BEGIN WITH SIMPLE HEAD SHAPES.

IT'S EASY TO COMPLETE THE DETAIL.

USE CIRCLES TO MAKE THE BODY.

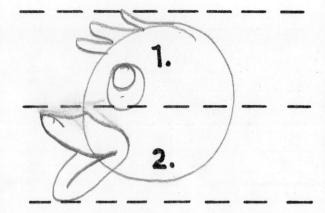

1.

2.

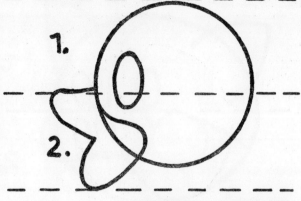

1.

2.

ADD LITTLE
FEATHERS,

AND
DETAILS
ON BILL.

ADD WEBBED FEET
SO HE CAN SWIM.

THE **PIG** STARTS WITH BASIC SHAPES.

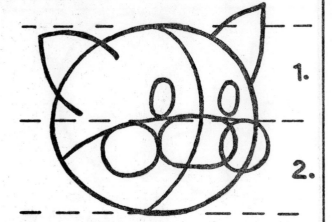

1.

2.

1.

2.

THE SNOUT AND CHEEK FOLLOW THE SAME LINE.

ADD A BIG SMILE.

THE BODY IS EASY!

THE **SHEEP** IS ALL CIRCLES AND OVALS.

ADD CURLY HAIR.

THE SHEEP KICKS UP ITS HEELS!

1.

2.

3.

1.

2.

3.

JUNGLE ANIMALS

_____

_____

_____

THE TIGER IS ALL OVALS AND CIRCLES.

THE TIGER HAS MANY MOODS. JUST CHANGE THE EYES AND MOUTH.

SCARED   MAD

HAPPY   SAD

1.

2.

3.

1.

2.

3.

A LONG TAIL.

DRAW THE TIGER'S BODY.
ADD DETAILS LIKE
WHISKERS AND STRIPES.

TAKE AWAY THE
STRIPES AND ADD A RUFF
AND YOU'VE DRAWN A
LION!

FOR THE **GIRAFFE**, USE A LARGE OVAL FOR THE HEAD.

THE GIRAFFE HAS BIG EYES AND SOFT HORNS.

AND SMALLER OVALS FOR EYES AND MOUTH.

ADD LONG EYELASHES, NOSE AND A SMILE.

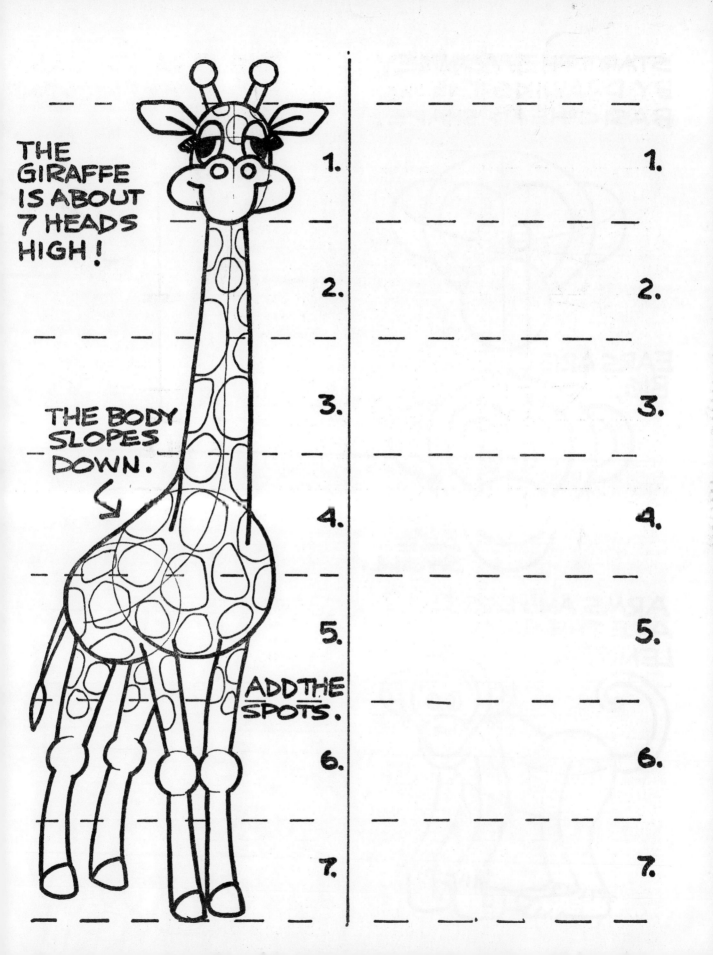

THE
GIRAFFE
IS ABOUT
7 HEADS
HIGH!

THE BODY
SLOPES
DOWN.

ADD THE
SPOTS.

1.

2.

3.

4.

5.

6.

7.

1.

2.

3.

4.

5.

6.

7.

START THE **MONKEY** BY DRAWING THE BASIC HEAD SHAPE.

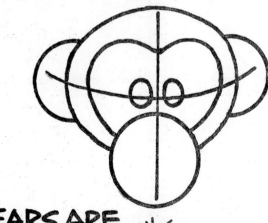

EARS ARE BIG,

EYES ARE SMALL.

ARMS AND LEGS ARE THE SAME LENGTH.

THE **HIPPO** IS FUN TO DRAW. START WITH THE BASIC SHAPES.

SMALL EARS, EYES AND A VERY BIG SMILE.

SHORT LEGS HOLD UP A BIG BODY!

THE ELEPHANT STARTS WITH A BOW TIE SHAPE.

ADD FAT CHEEKS.

THE TRUNK CAN GO UP, DOWN OR TO THE SIDE. DRAW A CURVED LINE IN THE DIRECTION YOU WANT.

ADD DETAILS.

MORE ELEPHANTS . . .

THIS ELEPHANT HAS TUSKS,

SHORT LEGS, BUT BIG FEET.

1.

2.

3.

1.

2.

3.

WATER ANIMALS

TO DRAW THE **FISH**, START WITH BASIC SHAPES.

HOW MANY FISH CAN YOU DRAW?

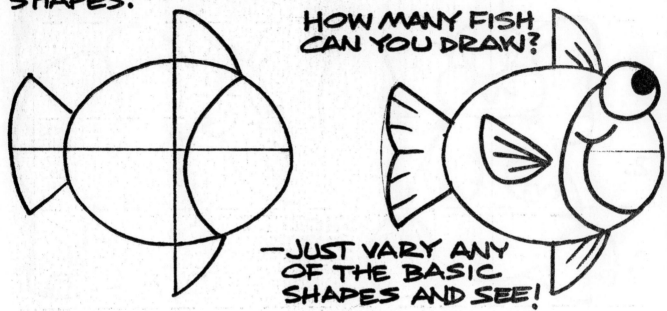

—JUST VARY ANY OF THE BASIC SHAPES AND SEE!

THE **WHALE'S** BASIC SHAPE
IS A LOT BIGGER THAN
THE FISH.

EYE IS BEHIND
THE MOUTH.

THE BIG OVAL
IS FLAT ON
THE BOTTOM.

ADD A VERY BIG
TAIL.

THE **SEAL** BEGINS
WITH 3 CIRCLES.

ADD A
MOUTH
AND
WHISKERS.

ADD 3 MORE
CIRCLES AND
YOU'VE GOT
THE BODY
AND A
BALL!

DON'T
FORGET
THE
FLIPPERS!

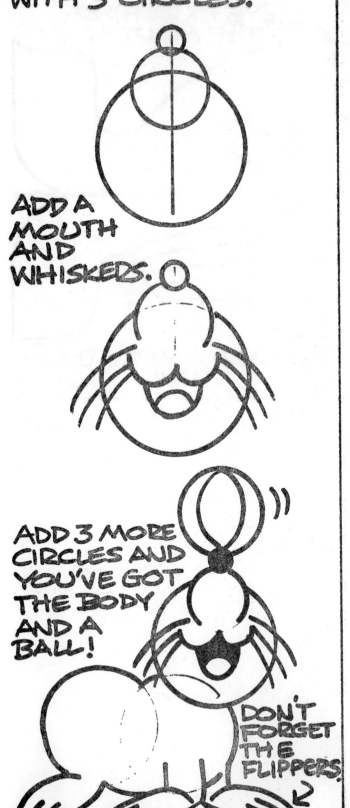

THE **OCTOPUS** IS FUN TO DRAW.

IT HAS A BIG HEAD AND 8 ARMS!

DRAW LINES FOR THE ARMS IN ANY DIRECTION.

ARMS ARE WIDE AT THE BODY AND NARROW AT THE TIP.

DRAW BIG EYES AND SUCTION CUPS.

TO DRAW A **FROG**, START WITH THE SIMPLE HEAD SHAPE.

HE HAS VERY LONG HIND LEGS

ADD BIG ROUND EYES,

AND WIDE OPEN MOUTH.

DRAW SHORT FRONT LEGS.

FROGS IN ACTION!

TO DRAW A SIDE VIEW, USE AN EGG SHAPE FOR THE HEAD AND LEGS.

A LEAP FROG.

FOREST ANIMALS

THE FOX BEGINS WITH A BASIC HEAD SHAPE.

THE EARS AND NOSE ARE VERY POINTED.

ADD A "FOXY" SMILE,

A SMALL BODY AND LONG TAIL.

1.

2.

1.

2.

TO DRAW THE **RABBIT,**
START WITH THE
BASIC HEAD SHAPE.

ADD VERY LONG
EARS,

AND A
BIG
FRONT
TOOTH.

THE RABBIT HAS A PEAR-
SHAPED BODY AND
LONG HIND FEET.

FRONT   REAR

1.

2.

1.

2.

TO DRAW THE BEAR,
START WITH THE
BASIC HEAD SHAPE.

ADD FUZZY EARS,
A BIG
NOSE,

AND
MOUTH.

THE BEARS BODY IS
BIG AND ROUND.

THE **CHIPMUNK** HAS AN EASY BASIC HEAD SHAPE.

ADD LITTLE POINTED EARS,

AND A LITTLE MOUTH WITH A BIG TOOTH.

JUST ADD A BIG FLUFFY TAIL TO THE BASIC BODY AND IT'S A **SQUIRREL**!

TO DRAW A **BIRD**,
BEGIN WITH THE
SIMPLE HEAD SHAPE.

ADD LITTLE
FEATHERS.

COMPLETE THE BILL
AND ADD BRIGHT EYES.

THE BODY IS FUN.
DRAW ACTION LINES
FOR THE WINGS
AND MAKE THE
BIRD FLY!

MORE PAGES
TO DRAW ON...